This Book Belongs to

_____

...a boy after God's own heart

A BOY
AFTER
GOD'S
OWN
HEART

JIM GEORGE

HARVEST HOUSE PUBLISHERS
EUGENE, OREGON

Cover by Garborg Design Works, Savage, Minnesota

Cover photos / illustrations © Bigstock / newyear 2008; Bigstock / Andrushko Galyna; Stockphoto / Taboga / Shutterstock / Monkey Business Images

A BOY AFTER GOD'S OWN HEART
Copyright © 2012 by Jim George
Published by Harvest House Publishers
Eugene, Oregon 97402
www.harvesthousepublishers.com

Library of Congress Cataloging-in-Publication Data
George, Jim, 1943-
    A boy after God's own heart / Jim George.
        p. cm.
    ISBN 978-0-7369-4502-8 (pbk.)
    ISBN 978-0-7369-4503-5 (eBook)
    1. Boys--Religious life--Juvenile literature. 2. Boys--Religious life--Textbooks. 3. Boys–Conduct of life--Juvenile literature. 4. Boys--Conduct of life--Textbooks. 5. Christian life–Juvenile literature. 6. Christian life--Textbooks. I. Title.
    BV4541.3.G45 2012
    248.8'2--dc23
                                                                    2012001364

14 15 16 17 18 19 20 / VP-KBD / 10 9 8 7 6 5 4

Contents

Acknowledgment

I want to thank my wife, Elizabeth,
for being the source of inspiration for some
of the material in this book. She paved the way
by writing a similar book for young girls.

Introduction
A Few Thoughts Before You Get Started

Hey there!

I'm Jim, and I'm so glad to meet you. And it's great that you are holding this book in your hands. I cannot tell you how excited I am that you and I are going to go on a journey together with Jesus. I've also invited a boy named Dylan to come along with us. He's a tween guy just like you who loves God and wants to follow Him.

As you prepare to make this exciting trip, here's a little information to get you started on your adventure.

Open your book

...and enjoy it. It's just a book! It's not homework. It's not assigned reading. It's not a chore. No, I wrote this book to be a fun adventure. Everything you need is here—except your favorite pen or pencil. I even put the Bible verses in the book for you. And if you have your own Bible handy, great!

Open your eyes

...to your friends. It will be so cool to go on this adventure with your best buddy and close guy friends! The more guys you get together, the merrier your adventure will be.

And if your dad is willing, you can ask him to go through the book with you.

...and pray. Ask Jesus to help you realize how much He loves you and wants to help you through life. Also, ask Him to show you what it means to be a boy after His own heart.

...and dream! Dream about your future. Dream about all the great things you want to do, like to do, and hope to do. You are very special, and it never hurts to dream your special dreams. They are a part of the wonderful person you are. I know you'll pick up lots of tips from this book that will help you live out your Number One dream—to be a boy after God's own heart.

Are you ready to let the fun begin? I am! As you read, please remember that every page of this book is covered with my prayers for you. And every word has been written with you in mind. I've tried to imagine what your day is like, and what would help you most as you get to know God and the Bible more. My hope is that through this book, you will become more and more a boy after God's own heart.

So—ready...set...here we go!

In Jesus' great and amazing love,

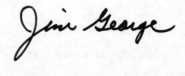

1

My Heart

"Dylan? Dylan! Dylan Douglas!" Mrs. Abrams called out. But Dylan was deep in thought. It wasn't until Dylan's friend Bart punched his arm that Dylan came back from the world of gaming. It took all his will to refocus his attention away from medieval knights and slaying dragons to the realization that he was at school and everyone was looking at him!

After a sheepish "Duh" followed by a blank stare, Mrs. Abrams, Dylan's English teacher, repeated her question.

You see, Dylan had become very distracted ever since he had started playing video games at Bart's house. Dylan was hooked. He couldn't stop thinking about battles and military strategy. He couldn't wait until school was over so he and Bart could ride off to Bart's house to play more games. Dylan and Bart's families were longtime friends, and it was understood that the two boys would work on homework together until Dylan's older sister, Helen, arrived from high school to take him home. But Dylan knew there was no way he and Bart were about to let a little schoolwork keep them from taking on their next gaming challenge!

Fun in God's Word!

There are many things in a guy's life that can distract his attention away from what is truly important. For Dylan, it was video games. They took his mind off his schoolwork—and everything else. He just couldn't stop thinking about all the cool fun he could have while playing video games.

So what's the problem? What's wrong with a video game? What's so bad about having some fun? Well, nothing! Especially if it's done after you've taken care of your responsibilities. And as long as it doesn't get out of hand or go to extremes. But Dylan's real problem was the focus of his heart. His was concerned with only one thing...Dylan! What he needed was a better understanding of where God wants His growing boys to focus their hearts.

I know that talking about your heart is not necessarily a "guy thing," but hang in there with me as we see why this is so important. Let's have some fun with the acrostic below that spells out H-E-A-R-T. Before you start, find a pen or pencil—and it's okay if it's a color like blue or red. Then, with your pen in hand, let's begin an adventure with Jesus and a trip into God's Word.

As you read the Bible verses in the following chapters, mark what you like and learn. And feel free to write all over your book! Along the way, try to answer the questions, even if only in your mind. And if you don't have a pen handy at all times or you only feel like reading, that's okay! I want reading this book to be fun—I don't want you to feel like this is another homework assignment.

So here we go! Say a prayer to God, and ask Him to work in your heart. Then let's take a moment to spell out H-E-A-R-T—God's way.

Have a heart checkup. Wow, was Jesus ever right on when He told the people who wanted to follow Him, "Where your treasure is, there your heart will be also" (Matthew 6:21). For Dylan, it's pretty obvious that his "treasure"—the focus of his heart—was on playing video games. For other boys, the focus of their hearts may be sports, or their desire to be part of the "in" crowd at school.

That brings us to the biggest, most important question of all: Where is *your* treasure? Where's *your* focus? Where's *your* heart? A boy after God's own heart wants to make sure his treasure—what he thinks is most valuable and important in the whole world—is what God says it should be.

As you begin this adventure in following Jesus and obeying Him, here's a key verse that shows you what God wants to be first in your life. It is Acts 13:22—and it's dynamite! In this verse God describes the heart of the man He chose to be king over His people. Here's what God says:

I have found David son of Jesse a man after My own heart; he will do everything I want him to do. What does a person after God's own heart do that sets him apart?

because he does what god not he wants !!!

My friend, this is the goal of this book—that you be growing into a boy after God's own heart, a boy who follows God and is willing to go on the adventure of doing whatever God wants you to do. Does this sound impossible? Well, it's not. Read on!

Experience God's love. Having a heart for God starts with realizing that He loves you. As much as your parents and grandparents love you, guess what? No one loves you more than God does. Let's look at what the Bible says about God's love:

> *God is love* (1 John 4:8). What do you learn about God in this verse?

_____

_____

_____

> *God so loved the world [including you!] that he gave his one and only Son, that whoever believes in him shall not perish but have eternal life* (John 3:16). Jesus, God's one and only Son, died for sinners. What does this tell you about how much God loves you?

A Boy After God's Own Heart

Allow God to guide you. Knowing God loves you requires a response from you. One key way you show your love for God is by doing what He wants you to do. Jesus tells us in the Bible how important it is to do His will. He said:

> *If you love me, you will obey what I command* (John 14:15). What does a heart that loves Jesus do?

_____

_____

_____

As we've already discovered, a boy after God's own heart is a boy who will do what God wants him to do. His thinking goes like this: "If God wants me to do this, I am going to do it. And if God doesn't want me to do this, I'm sure not going to do it!"

Are you wondering, "How? How can I know what God wants me to do? How can I be sure of what He wants?" Well, I have some great news for you! God has already told you His will in His Word, the Bible. So be sure you take some time each day to read your Bible. If you don't understand what you are reading or you have questions, ask your parents, pastor, or Sunday school teacher. God has given these people to you to guide you and help you understand what God wants you to do, how He wants you to act, and the choices He wants you to make.

Your word is a lamp to my feet and a light to my path (Psalm 119:105). How does this verse say the Bible will help you?

_____

_____

_____

I have hidden your word in my heart that I might not sin against you (Psalm 119:11). How will learning and memorizing God's Word help you?

_____

_____

_____

Remember, God wants you to love Him. Think about some of the things you love. I hope your mom and dad pop into your mind as people you love. And maybe a younger brother or sister. Perhaps you even thought of your dog, or a hobby like Legos, building models, or playing computer games. Or maybe you really like playing sports like baseball or soccer, or going swimming or to the beach. Or even things you love to eat like ice cream, chocolate candy, chips, and donuts. (Help—I'm getting hungry!)

Take a few minutes to make your own list of "Things I Love":

_____

_____

_____

_____

Now—back to God! God wants you to love *Him*. In fact, He wants to be at the top of your "Things I Love" list. He wants you to love Him more than all others things. And He wants you to love Him with all your heart. Jesus says,

Love the Lord your God with all your heart and with all your soul and with all your mind (Matthew 22:37). Circle every time the word "all" is used.

Love like this is a tall order, isn't it? But it is possible to love God more than anything else. All you have to do is choose to put Him first in your life and in your heart, one day at a time. Here are some ways to get started:

★ When you go to bed at night, tell God that you love Him and that you are going to think about Him first thing as soon as you wake up. Then say, "Good night, Lord. I love You."

★ When you wake up, say, "Good morning" to God. It's just like King David said in Psalm 5:3: "My voice

You shall hear in the morning, O LORD" (NKJV). Thank the Lord for His love, for His blessings, for all the good things in your life, and for a new day.

★ You know what people do when they want to remember something, don't you? They write it down. If you haven't been doing it already, why not start writing down some things you don't want to forget. Especially things you learn about God and Jesus and their love for you. Try it! Then when you are getting ready for bed at night, say, "Thank You" to God for all the wonderful things He gave you in just this one day!

Take the temperature of your heart. In this book we'll talk a lot about your heart—that part of you that feels happiness or sadness, that part of you that has wants and feelings. So let's start by taking the temperature of your heart. You already know about how your mom or dad takes your temperature with a thermometer when you're not feeling well. That helps your parents to know if you are sick or not. And, if you are sick, your temperature helps them know if you are just a little sick or *really* sick!

With that in mind, let's look at this scene from the book of Revelation, the last book in the Bible. Jesus is speaking to the people in a certain church. Here's what He said to them:

I know your deeds, that you are neither cold nor hot. I wish you were either one or the other! So, because you are lukewarm—neither hot nor cold—I am about to spit you out of my mouth (Revelation 3:15-16). In those words, Jesus mentions three heart conditions or temperatures. List them here:

_____

_____

_____

To be *coldhearted* means to be unemotional, to be unaware of God. It is hard to imagine being a person who doesn't even think about God at all. To be *lukewarm* means to be indifferent and bored. Imagine being numb toward God, bored about God. That's horrible! And the third temperature—*hot*—means that the heat of your heart and your emotions toward God is sky-high. That means your heart for God is boiling over with excitement. It's what is often called "a fiery love." It describes the heart of someone—hopefully you!—who loves God and is committed to Him.

What is the reading on your heart's thermometer? Or, put another way, what is the level of your feelings toward God? It is hot, lukewarm, or cold? Be honest. God already knows, so let Him know that you know! Then you and He can work together to do something about it.

Straight Talk About Your Heart

Just think about Jesus' love for a minute. He loved you so much that He died for you on the cross so you could have eternal life and live with Him forever. And think about how He loved you before you ever loved Him. That's what the Bible says: *God demonstrates his own love for us in this: While we were still sinners, Christ died for us* (Romans 5:8).

I hope your heart is as excited about Jesus right now as mine is. And I hope it's a fiery excitement. And if it's not, I hope your heart will warm up, ignite, and burn with a real love for Jesus.

All sorts of exciting and positive things happen when you turn up the heat of your love for Jesus. So let's discover how you can understand a bit more about Jesus and His plan for you. But first, pray this prayer. Use these words to tell Jesus about your desire to know and love Him more and more.

A Prayer to Pray
Dear Jesus, help me
to love You more,
to know You better,
and to follow You
with all my heart.
Amen.

★ TRAVELING WITH JESUS ★

In this chapter we had some fun in God's Word learning about the importance of your **H-E-A-R-T**. On this page, write out the point for each letter. (I'll get you started with "H.")

H—Have a heart checkup

E_____

A_____

R_____

T_____

Now, write out one thing you liked, learned, or want to do about your heart and your love for Jesus. Then enjoy the journey!

_____

_____

_____

_____

_____

_____

2

My Space

Yes!" Dylan pumped the air with his fist. "It's Saturday!" Then a second later, Dylan muttered, "Oh no. It's Saturday!" Maybe this seems like a strange thing for a boy who loved his Saturdays to say. But as Dylan had gotten older, Saturdays had become a mixed blessing.

On one hand, Dylan loved spending time on Saturdays hanging out with his best bud and neighbor, Bart. Today they had a big day planned. But on the other hand, Saturday was the day he was supposed to clean his room. Dylan's mom reminded him every single day to keep his room neat and his stuff put away. But Dylan was usually too busy—or late—to tidy his room. So by the time Saturday arrived, his room was messy.

And Dylan dreaded the moment when, on Saturday morning, his mom would barge into his "Bat Cave" in a flurry and order him to get up and get busy *right now*! She would tell him to pick up his clothes, books, CDs, and video games...not to mention his trash!

"Ugh!" was all Dylan could manage as he glumly looked around his room. Piles of wadded clothes were everywhere. As he waded through the sea of T-shirts, socks, blue jeans, gym clothes, and of course all the other things that were piled up including school papers, video games, and candy wrappers, he noticed his prize T-shirt that had been MIA (Missing In Action) for several weeks.

"Eureka!" he shouted. "There you are!" he grinned as he reached down to retrieve his lost prize. "The lost has been found," he said, gleefully quoting a verse from the Bible.

Fun in God's Word!

Why is it that we guys like to live in chaos and messiness? I'm sure you've watched your mom working hard to take care of the place where you and your family live. And I bet your dad keeps his tools and workbench neat and tidy. Well, you can and should do the same thing for your own room or the part of the room that you share with one or more of your siblings. You may find this hard to believe, but when you take care of your part of the house—whether it is your bunk in the bedroom or a bedroom all your own—you'll feel really great about it. And here's a bonus—you'll get into the habit of staying well organized for the future God has planned for you.

To find out what a few of those plans are, get your hands on a pen again. It's time to mark what you learn in the verses below about your space—your personal place of retreat. Once again, we'll spell it out—S-P-A-C-E.

A Boy After God's Own Heart

Show good character by taking care of your **space.** Remember our theme verse? It's Acts 13:22. A boy who wants to follow God is one who wants what God wants. He wants to do God's will. And he wants to please God. Did you ever think that a part of God's plan for you is learning to take care of your space? That's right! The Bible says,

> *Whatever you do, work at it with all your heart, as working for the Lord, not for men* (Colossians 3:23). At your age, you don't have a job like an adult does. But you do have your room. That—and helping around the house—is your job. And you show good character qualities when you take care of your room and help around the house. How does this verse say you are to do your work, including taking care of your clothes and your stuff?

_____

_____

_____

Who does this verse say you are working for?

_____

_____

_____

Pray and thank Jesus for your space. Like Dylan, your space is special to you. It's your place, your hideaway. So take some time to describe your room in the lines below. When you're done, don't forget to thank Jesus for all the things you have and for a place and space of your own. The Bible says, "Be thankful" (Colossians 3:15).

_____

_____

_____

_____

_____

_____

Acknowledge your duty. You can do lots of things with your time—watch TV, play video games, play soccer with your friends. But there's something else that requires your time—your room! And God is asking you to take care of this special place. He says:

> *If a man is lazy, the rafters sag; if his hands are idle, the house leaks* (Ecclesiastes 10:18). What does the Bible call a man who fails to take care of his home?

_____

_____

_____

Obviously you aren't in charge of your home. That is your parents' responsibility. But think for a minute, and then write down how the verse above applies to you and your space, or your room.

_____

_____

_____

_____

_____

Clean freaks apply here. Whatever you do, don't freak out as we talk about being a clean freak. Just think about this for a minute. Your room is you. If it's tidy, that tells people something about you and your character, or what kind of person you are. It tells people you are a neat and responsible person. And if your space is a real pigpen, that sends a completely different message about yourself. What you want to be is neat and organized.

Take a look at the chart on the next page. First, I want you to circle every time the word "your" appears in the chart. Next, make a check mark in the column that represents the person who usually does each of the following basic chores. If it's another person ("other"), write in that person's name for each task he or she does. When you're done, add up the check marks to see who's really taking care of your room.

TASK	YOU	MOM	OTHER
Make your bed			
Vacuum your floor			
Hang up your clothes			
Put away your clean clothes			
Pick up your dirty clothes			
Put away your stuff			
Total of check marks	____	____	_____

Now look at your totals. What do they tell you? Who's doing most of *your* work?

Here's a challenge. Try being a "neat freak" for a few days. And be prepared—you'll probably have to pick your mom up off the floor during those few days! But I guarantee, you'll be proud of the results. You'll feel good about your room—and yourself. Why? Because you'll realize that *you*—not your mom or an older brother or sister—made your room neat and a great place to be. Here's a thought from God about being tidy and neat:

Everything should be done in...[an] orderly way (1 Corinthians 14:40). This verse gives you a general principle for life, including the way you live and take care of your things. What does it say about order and about being a neat freak?

_____

_____

Enjoy your space. When it comes to your room, I realize your mom probably has a lot to say about your furniture and sheets, and especially what you hang on the walls. Don't forget, God wants you to listen to her and respect her.

There are good reasons why your mom says yes or no to your ideas. For instance, stuff for your room costs money. A wall that has holes in it from posters and pictures has to be patched and painted later on. And if your parents are renting the house you live in, the person who owns the house might have rules about what your family is allowed (and not allowed) to do with the walls and paint colors of your home.

What can you do? Realize you need to work *with* your mom and dad when it comes to making changes in your room. Share your ideas about what you think would look cool. Pay attention when your parents share their decorating advice. When it comes to their help, instruction, and advice about your room (or *anything!*), the Bible has something to say to you:

> *Listen, my son...and do not forsake your mother's teaching. They* [her teachings] *are a garland to grace your head and a chain to adorn your neck* (Proverbs 1:8-9). Who is a great person to teach you about taking care of your room?

_____

_____

_____

_____

Straight Talk About Your Heart

Did you ever think that the God of the universe would be interested in you and the things you do and don't do? Well, amazingly, He is! God is totally interested in how you take care of your room, how you manage your space. As you follow God in this area, get ready for a b-i-g reward! When you look at your clean room, at all your neat things and your stuff in order, you will be proud of your efforts. You will be glad you followed God's instructions to take care of what you have. And, as a big bonus, your parents will be pleased!

A Prayer to Pray
Dear Jesus, I see how important
my character is to You
and to my parents.
I want to do a better job
of taking care of
my room and my stuff.
Amen.

★ TRAVELING WITH JESUS ★

In this chapter we had some fun in God's Word learning about the importance of taking care of your **S-P-A-C-E.** On this page, write out the point for each letter. (I'll get you started with "S.")

S—show good character by taking care of your space

P_____

A_____

C_____

E_____

Now, write out one thing you liked, learned, or want to do about your space. Then enjoy the journey!

_____

_____

_____

_____

_____

_____

My Space

3

My Parents

"D ylan? Dylan! Dylan Douglas!" Oh boy, here we go again! Dylan was staring out the window at school—again. But this time he wasn't lost in thought about a video game. No, this was way more serious. He was thinking about how much he missed his dad.

Now, before you get the wrong idea, understand that Mr. Douglas is alive and well! What Dylan was missing was time with his dad. Recently, his dad had been sent by his company to India to open a new office. He would be gone for six months...and so far he had been gone only one week, which meant Dylan would be without his dad for another 23 weeks! Dylan was already feeling a deep void in his life. They had been best buddies, playing video games, wrestling on the living room floor, playing catch in the front yard, and getting ice cream together.

Yes, things had definitely changed. For instance, Dylan's mom had a lot more work to do now that his dad wasn't at home to help. And his mom just didn't seem to have much time for him as she focused on his younger sister and a sister in high school. As a result, Dylan felt sad—and mad!

He felt like he had lost his best friend. He didn't like it, and his attitude was bad. He was even beginning to talk back to his mom. Dylan had always been eager to please and obey his parents, but his bitterness and confusion were causing him to sulk and refuse to follow even the simplest requests from his mother.

Maybe your dad isn't gone from home six months at a time, but he's still gone a lot. Maybe his job requires him to travel every week. Or perhaps your father is a missionary who leaves for a month at a time. Or maybe he is an executive for his company and his job takes him to other countries or to lots of meetings. Whatever the case, I'm sure it hurts when your dad has to be gone. That means you love him and he loves you. And that's a good thing, because God wants you to love your dad.

Fun in God's Word!

You probably hear lots of kids put their parents down, criticize them, and make fun of them. You've probably even heard them say things like, "My parents are so stupid. What do they know anyway?"

If you listen too much to this kind of talk, you'll begin to think that is how you are supposed to talk about your parents. I heard a lot of this when I was growing up. And I still hear a lot of it now. But I remember the day I looked at James 1:17, which says, "Every good and perfect gift is from above, coming down from the Father." With my parents in mind, I then realized, "Wait a minute! God gave me my parents exactly the way they are and who they are. That means they are one of His gifts to me!"

I can't begin to tell you how this truth from God changed my attitude toward my parents. Instead of seeing them as goofy, old-fashioned, too strict, and picky, I started seeing them as special gifts from God, just for me. And God wants you to have this same attitude about your mom and dad.

Let's have some fun as we spell out P-A-R-E-N-T-S. Get your pen or pencil ready, and let your adventure into God's Word continue!

Pray for your parents. Prayer is a wonderful habit. No matter where you are or what's happening, you can always talk to God. God cares about you, and guess what? He cares about your parents too. Praying for your mom or dad is a good thing. It helps you to love and care about them even more. You can even make a special page in a journal or diary (if you have one) just for the prayers you want to say for your dad and mom.

> *Always [give] thanks to God the Father for everything* (Ephesians 5:20). What is God telling you to do here? When are you to do it? Have you given thanks to God for your parents recently? If not, why not now?

_____

_____

_____

Always remember that giving thanks is a part of prayer. So don't forget to thank God every day for your very own special parents.

And don't forget to say thank you to your parents every day, all day long, for everything. Your parents do a lot for you. Whenever they buy you some new clothes, tell them thank you. If they take you to music lessons, or they give you a uniform for your sports team, say thank you. When they give you a meal, say thank you. When clean clothes magically show up in your drawers, say thank you. And when you go to bed, say, "Thanks, Mom—or thanks, Dad—for another great day!"

Ask their advice. God gave you your parents. And guess what? They can help you make good decisions, give you great advice, and guide you in the right direction. They have wisdom to share. (Yes, they too had to grow up!) And most of all, they love you and want the best for you. No one loves you more than your parents do—except for God, of course!

Once your parents give you advice or make a rule or a decision, it is important for you to do what they say. (Even if you think you have a better idea!) One day right after I got my driver's license I asked my dad if I could take the car out and ride around with some of my friends. My dad said no—he said I wasn't quite ready to go out on my own. Well, you guessed it. I just knew that he was wrong! So when he left for a business trip, I took the car out for a spin, literally, and ended up getting a big gash in the side of the car.

My dad was definitely right! I wasn't ready to drive on my own, and especially with a bunch of my friends. In my pride, I started showing off at the steering wheel, and I ended up wrecking the car. That was a hard and painful lesson to learn!

Usually, if your attitude is right, you can talk things over with your parents. You can ask them why they made a certain decision. You can ask them what you need to do to earn a privilege. In the end, though, you want to do what they say—and do it with a happy heart.

> *Listen, my [child], to your father's instruction and do not forsake your mother's teaching* (Proverbs 1:8). What is God's advice regarding your father and your mother?

_____

_____

_____

Respect your parents. Think for a minute about your teachers at school. You answer when they call on you. You do whatever they ask. And you wouldn't dare argue with them.

Well, why would you show such respect for teachers you see for only a few hours each week, and choose *not* to treat your parents the same way? Why would you submit to authority at school, but not at home? Once again, Jesus has something to say about this:

Honor your father and mother (Matthew 15:4). What is Jesus' clear and simple command to you?

_____

_____

_____

Maybe you already know that when Jesus said these words, He was talking about one of the Ten Commandments. That makes this instruction from God really important to remember, doesn't it?

So, what does it mean to respect your parents? It means to treat them politely and with honor. It means to admire them. It means to listen when they talk. It means to accept their decisions, follow their rules, and seek to please them. And it means you don't talk back or argue!

Experience God's blessing by obeying your parents. I'm sure you have great ideas about the way you want to do things. So how can you know if what you want to do is the right thing to do? Well, God did not leave you to make decisions on your own. He gave you your parents to help you make the right choices at each stage of your life. And when you follow your parents' guidance and rules, you will experience God's blessing. These verses tell you how. (And don't miss the promise that goes with the blessing!)

Children, obey your parents in the Lord, for this is right (Ephesians 6:1). What is God's command to you? Why should you obey your parents?

_____

_____

_____

Honor your father and mother...that it may go well with you (Ephesians 6:2-3). What is God's command to you, and what is one result of doing this?

_____

_____

_____

Never criticize your parents to others. God wants you to love, honor, and respect your father and mother. So be careful not to criticize them. Don't put them down or make fun of them when you talk to other people. Instead, speak well of your parents. No matter how popular it is for kids to talk badly about their parents, you shouldn't. Why?

A foolish [person] despises his mother (Proverbs 15:20). To despise means to mock and to have no respect. How does God describe a son or daughter who despises their mother?

_____

_____

_____

Trust God. It takes trust in God to listen to your parents and do what they say. You have to trust that God is leading and growing you through your parents. No matter what happens, you can always trust God.

> *Trust in the LORD with all your heart and lean not on your own understanding; in all your ways acknowledge him, and he will make your paths straight* (Proverbs 3:5-6). What is God's promise to you if you will trust and follow Him "with all your heart"?

_____

_____

_____

_____

_____

Say, "I love you." Isn't it great when your parents say, "I love you" or show their love to you? And you love them as much as they love you, right? So why not tell them you love them—often? Just say, "Love ya, Mom!" Make it a habit. And love isn't just the words you say. It's also action and behavior. Read on!

Dear children, let us not love with words or tongue but with actions and in truth (1 John 3:18). In addition to saying, "I love you," how do you prove you love your parents?

_____

_____

_____

Straight Talk About Your Heart

Let's go back to Dylan again. Remember how confused and upset he was with his dad being gone so much? So what did Dylan do? He began to do things like not obeying his mother and not showing respect.

Now, think about this. Who was Dylan hurting? For sure, he was probably hurting his mom. And if his dad had seen the way he was acting, his dad would have been hurt too. But according to what you just learned from the Bible, who else would be disappointed? *God* is the right answer.

A boy after God's own heart follows God's instruction to honor his parents. Think about the key verse for this book—Acts 13:22: "I have found David son of Jesse a man after My own heart; he will do everything I want him to do."

This verse tells us that a boy after God's own heart will do everything God wants him to do. If you have been mean or hateful to your parents, it is definitely time for a change of heart. Tell God what's been going on. Then ask for His forgiveness. Tell Him you are sorry and ask for His help. And tell Him you want to follow His Word and love, honor, and obey your parents.

And then take the final step—do it! Make the changes you need to make. You can do it, because God will help you do it. Pray and work on having a happy, obedient heart in all things, and see what a radical difference respecting your parents makes at home.

A Prayer to Pray
Lord, I really need
Your help on this one!
Help me to grow up
enough to not only obey
my parents, but to love
and listen to them.
Amen.

★ TRAVELING WITH JESUS ★

In this chapter we had some fun in God's Word learning about the importance of **P-A-R-E-N-T-S**. On this page, write out the point for each letter. (I'll get you started with "P.")

P—Pray for your parents

A_____

R_____

E_____

N_____

T_____

S_____

Now, write out one thing you liked, learned, or want to do about being a better son. Then enjoy the journey!

_____

_____

_____

_____

_____

4

My Family

"Get out of my room, you little brat!" yelled Helen, Dylan's older sister. You wouldn't think that being five years apart in age would make that much difference, but Dylan and Helen seemed to be from different planets!

Besides being a girl, Helen was into clothes, music, friends, and especially boys. "What could she possibly see in that Bruce guy?" was the constant question on Dylan's mind as he would often sneak a peek of Helen and Bruce holding hands at the front door. Yuck! The guy looked like really bad news. And Dylan told Helen this over and over.

Maybe that was why Helen had determined to take every opportunity to be mean to Dylan. Whenever Helen was around, Dylan couldn't seem to do anything right. Helen considered herself the princess of the family, and Dylan was there to serve her—or else get out of her way!

Yes, Dylan felt like he was living in the Dark Ages and he was a serf or slave in some castle doing the bidding of the evil Queen Helen. Why did Helen have to be so hateful? Why couldn't they just be friends—like Bart and his sister?

Fun in God's Word!

It's pen or pencil time again! Now we're going on an adventure to discover what God tells us about our family members. As you have fun with the acrostic below that spells out F-A-M-I-L-Y, keep your pen handy. As you read, ask God for some good ideas about being a better family member.

Family is first. There is nothing as special as a family. Over the years your friends will come and go, but you will always have your family. And believe it or not, the day will come when you and your brothers and sisters will actually get along with each other and want to spend lots of time together.

Since family is your top priority (after God, that is), you need to make a decision to be true and loyal to your siblings. You can support your little sis in her soccer or gymnastics. The same is true for a big sister's swim meets or piano recitals. And after the game or activity, don't forget to tell them what a great job they did. Or, if they didn't get to play or it didn't go so well, give them a pat on the back and say, "I'm still proud of you. What you are doing isn't easy. Your day will come." Be supportive in as many ways as you can.

A friend loves at all times, and a brother is born for adversity (Proverbs 17:17). Now read this verse again and say or think the word "brother" instead of "friend." This verse is telling you how important family is when someone is suffering. How often is a brother to love his family? When especially is a brother to support his family members? Even when things get tough, what is God asking of you as a brother, son, and family member?

_____

_____

_____

_____

Ask God for help. It's hard to understand, but praying for others, including a mean, stuck-up older sister, changes you. It's easy to fight with or yell at your brother or sister. It's easy to say mean things to them. And it's easy to call them names. But God wants something better from you. He wants you to pray instead of fighting and yelling.

Praying for family members can be hard—especially if your feelings have been hurt, or you have been ignored or treated badly. But go ahead and ask God to help you love them, no matter what. Ask Him to help you be kind, even when they are mean. It's hard to pray for others and hate them at the same time. Soon you will discover you have a little more patience with them and your feelings are turning to love and concern.

Here is some advice from Jesus that will help you with your heart:

I tell you: Love your enemies and pray for those who persecute you (Matthew 5:44). What are the two steps Jesus asks of you?

★ _____

★ _____

Mean attitudes must go. I'm sure you have been on the receiving end of jokes, teasing, and name-calling. Well, you can't control what others say and do, but you are totally in control of what *you* say and do! You can choose to be mean and make fun of others—or not. You can decide to laugh at others and put them down—or not. And guess what? The best place to start being nice is at home, with your very own family.

You can't make others be nice to you or to each other, but you can be sure *you* don't act in the wrong ways to others. You can make sure you don't hurt your brothers and sisters through your words or actions. Instead, you can help your brothers and sisters feel better. God says:

Do not let any unwholesome talk come out of your mouths, but only what is helpful for building others up (Ephesians 4:29). What are God's rules for your mouth and what you say to others?

★ Do not speak what is...

★ Do speak what is...

★ Why?

A Boy After God's Own Heart

Initiate a change in your attitude. There is a scary story in the Old Testament about two brothers, Cain and Abel. Cain was angry with his brother because God liked Abel's offering better than Cain's offering. Listen in now on God's talk with Cain about his attitude:

> *The LORD said to Cain, "Why are you angry?...sin is crouching at your door; it desires to have you, but you must master it"* (Genesis 4:6-7). How did God describe Cain's anger? What did God tell him to do about his angry attitude?

_____

_____

_____

Now here's the scary part. Cain did not do what God said to do. Cain did not change his attitude. Instead, "Cain attacked his brother Abel and killed him" (verse 8). God's message to your heart is this: The next time you get mad at a brother or sister, remember what God told Cain. And do what God told Cain to do—control your bad attitude before it controls you!

Love your brothers and sisters, no matter what. When it comes to love, Dylan had the right idea. Even though Helen was mean to him, Dylan still loved his older sister and wanted to be friends with her. Dylan's feelings were not based on any nice things Helen did for him.

In fact, it was just the opposite. In spite of Helen's actions, Dylan still loved her and cared about her.

How about you? Do you have this kind of love for your family members, especially your brothers and sisters? It's the kind of love God wants you to have, a love that is not based on the actions of others, but a love that comes from God's love for you. Take a look at this verse:

> *A new command I give you: Love one another. As I have loved you, so you must love one another* (John 13:35). Love is so important to God that He commands us to love each other, especially our brothers and sisters. How—and how much—does Jesus say you are to love your family members?

_____

_____

_____

Your response to your family is important to God. Are you beginning to see a theme in this acrostic of F-A-M-I-L-Y? *You* are in control of your attitudes. *You* can be nice and sweet—or you can be hateful and hurtful. The choice is all yours.

Do you remember how we talked about speaking well of your parents in a previous chapter? We learned how important it is that you not talk about them in a negative or bad way, that you not put them down or make fun of them to others. Well, the same is true about your brothers and sisters. You can respond to them with kindness and love. And you can speak well of them to others. That's what God wants you to do.

Be kind and compassionate to one another, forgiving each other, just as in Christ God forgave you (Ephesians 4:32). List three actions and attitudes you are to have toward others, including your brothers and sisters.

★ _____

★ _____

★ _____

Straight Talk About Your Heart

Family members should adopt the motto of the Three Musketeers—"All for one and one for all." How can you help to make your home a better place for your family? It starts with you being a son and a brother who is there for his parents and brothers and sisters. It starts with you thinking of others, encouraging others, and loving your family members. So make your move!

Got a big brother? Write him a note of thanks for being a super big brother and slip it under his door. Got a big sister? See if there is anything you can help her with in her busy schedule. Got a little brother? Help him, play with him, laugh with him, hug him, and encourage him. Got a little sister? Get involved in her life. Say, "Want to play?" or "Here, let me help you with that."

Now, here's a thought: Maybe you are the older brother. Are you being God's helpful, kind big bro? You saw what happened when an older sibling, Helen, was so involved with herself that she failed to notice how much Dylan wanted her to like him. I hope and pray you aren't living in your own world so much that you ignore your younger siblings. A boy after God's own heart is also a brother after God's own heart. What can you do today to love your brothers and sisters?

A Prayer to Pray
Dear Jesus, this is another area
where I really need Your help!
Give me more love for my family,
especially my brothers and sisters.
Amen.

★ TRAVELING WITH JESUS ★

In this chapter we had some fun in God's Word learning about the importance of **F-A-M-I-L-Y.** On this page, write out the point for each letter. (I'll get you started with "F.")

F—Family is first

A_____

M_____

I_____

L_____

Y_____

Now, write out one thing you liked, learned, or want to do about your heart and your relationship with your family. Then enjoy the journey!

_____

_____

_____

_____

_____

5

My School

School. (Oh boy, here we go!) When it came to school, Dylan was neutral. Totally neutral. He could take it or leave it. Sure, he liked the first day of school, the day before a vacation like Thanksgiving, Christmas, and spring break, and of course the final day of school, before summer break. Everything else Dylan tolerated.

But today, as he kicked at some rocks on the road that led to his neighborhood school, Dylan was not happy at all. He had to admit, though, that he really did like Mr. Adams's science class. In fact, Dylan couldn't wait each day to see what neat new experiment Mr. Adams would come up with next. This class was the coolest thing in Dylan's world. Whatever projects Mr. Adams asked the class to do, Dylan rushed with excitement to do his best.

But beyond his favorite teacher and his favorite subject, science, Dylan wasn't that thrilled about school. To him, math was hard. History was boring. English seemed like a waste of time. After all, didn't he already speak English?

Then Dylan's thoughts went to the only other bright spot in his school day—his physical education class. He loved PE, especially when he got to play baseball when the weather was nice. Otherwise he was a bit short for basketball, and volleyball wasn't his game either.

And after school? All that homework—ugh! All Dylan wanted to do when he got home was kick back and relax with a snack and some down time in front of the TV. Or ride bikes around the neighborhood with Bart and some of his other neighborhood buddies. But his most favorite after-school activity was to go to Bart's house and play video games. Bart had every action game you could possibly imagine! Dylan couldn't help but dream about the future, about when he would be an adult and could sit around and play video games all that he wanted. "Boy, I can hardly wait!" he thought to himself.

Dylan's thoughts turned back to reality as he looked up to see the school building looming ahead. (Why, he wondered, did it look like a prison?) "I sure hope Mr. Adams has a fun experiment planned for today," Dylan thought. "Otherwise I'm in for another really l-o-n-g day!"

Fun in God's Word!

I think all young guys look forward to being older, especially old enough to drive a car! Maybe that is why we love birthdays—all those presents, and the bonus of being a little older and more grown-up. But with each year of growth comes more responsibility, like taking school more seriously. School is an important part of growing up. It requires dedication, commitment, and time. But it can also be exciting and fun!

I want you to have some fun now with the acrostic below that spells out S-C-H-O-O-L. Before we begin, here's something to remember if you're struggling with school and schoolwork—you can ask God for an attitude change.

See school as a training ground for life. Whether you attend public school, a private school, or you are home-schooled, school is made up of lots of different things. The physical location and the time you spend there provide many opportunities for your growth. Just think about the many great skills you develop:

★ At school you have opportunities to talk to and work with teachers, classmates, and friends.

★ At school you learn how to ask and answer questions, give reports and presentations, and talk to a group.

★ At school you also learn to think and find solutions to problems and challenges.

★ At school you learn to act in a proper way toward those in authority and toward your fellow students. Also, being in school teaches you to restrain your emotions—and your mouth!—and to focus your active mind and energy.

Are you getting a better understanding about why school is so important? I hope so. Here's something from the Bible to help you with your attitude toward school.

If you look for [wisdom] as for silver and search for it as for hidden treasure, then you will understand the fear of the LORD and find the knowledge of God (Proverbs 2:4-5). Circle the words that describe the wealth and value of wisdom. Then underline the words that describe what you must do to get wisdom and knowledge. What is the result of gaining wisdom?

_____

_____

_____

_____

Check your attitude. Have you ever heard the saying, "Attitude is everything"? Well, it sure seemed to apply to Dylan when it came to his attitude about school. No matter where you go to school, you can make your time there whatever you want it to be. It can be fun and exciting, something you can look back on in the future with good memories—or it can be a living nightmare. And the amazing thing is that *you* get to choose which it will be!

Your happiness and success in school begin with your attitude. Can you say, "I'm going to make my school years fun, exciting, and meaningful"? I have a favorite quote I want to pass on to you. It says, "Wherever you are, be all there." Since you have to "be" at school, why not decide to "be all there"? Maybe this Bible verse will help.

A Boy After God's Own Heart

Whatever you do, work at it with all your heart, as working for the Lord, not for men (Colossians 3:23). How are you to do all your work, including going to school?

_____

_____

_____

_____

_____

Homework is a priority. Of course, God is your Number One priority. Just think about it: Your whole life involves Him and revolves around Him. He is to be the most important person or thing in your life.

And one of God's major priorities for you is for you to learn and grow by going to school and doing your homework. God's will for you at this time in your life is to be a student—to go to school, to learn as much as you can.

If you're like most of the guys I know, getting started on anything—including doing your homework—is the hardest part of any task. There just seem to be so many more exciting things to do! But you can't *finish* your homework until you *start* doing it. God has a few hints on how to do this— and with the right attitude!

Make every effort to add to your faith goodness; and to goodness, knowledge; and to knowledge, self-control, and to self-control, perseverance (2 Peter 1:5-6). What do the first three words in these verses say is the very first thing you must do to move forward in your maturity, which includes things like your homework?

_____

_____

_____

_____

As you can see, growth requires something from you—effort and hard work! And the effort you make will pay off big time as one good quality after another becomes a part of your life.

Organize for success. School is a place for learning. But to learn well, you need to be organized. One thing you'll need to do for better success in school is set up a special place for doing your homework. Of course, you'll want your mom's approval of the place you pick. And you will also need her help. But wherever it is, try to make it a place you want to be. Think about special pencils and pens—and cool erasers! Ask your mom for a timer or clock to help you work faster, stay focused, finish your homework by a certain time, and even play "beat the clock."

Next, pick and schedule a time for doing your homework. And here's a hint for success—try to make it the same time each day. The smart guys (not IQ smart, but smart with their time) do some of their homework while they're at the bus stop. Or while they're waiting on the steps at school for their ride home. Or while they're at their grandmother's house while mom is on her way home from work. Or even while sitting around the kitchen table all morning long with brothers and sisters while they're being home-schooled. Whatever works for you and your family, that will be your time. And here's another hint—sooner is better! Challenge yourself to do your "work" (as in homework) first. Then play games, watch TV, or go outside to play ball.

I have been able to do a lot of things in my life. I am a pharmacist, a soldier, a pastor, a missionary, a teacher, and now a writer. How did all of this happen? Not by playing video games all the time, or daydreaming about how much fun I would have if I could just get through school. Take my writing, for example. I have now written 15 books—and this book is number 16. These books didn't just get written on their own. They happened because every day over the years, I have gone to my desk (my place where all my favorite things are) at a certain time (my time). Then I stay there until I have written five pages.

In other words, it's just like when I used to do homework as a kid. I learned from doing homework every day *how* to get things done.

My wife has a best friend, Judy, who is an artist. Judy has illustrated three of my books for boys. These illustrations are actually 30 of her paintings. So far, Judy has created about 100 paintings. How did she make that happen?

Every day she goes to her work space (her place where all her neat art supplies are) at a certain time (her time). Then she stays there until she has done her work for the day.

My young friend, I will tell you that the years and years—and years!—of doing homework in a certain place at a certain time prepared both Judy and me for what we do now.

Other stuff is part of school. School offers many opportunities to get involved in different activities like sports or music. Maybe you're not so good at basketball, like Dylan, or running races, but maybe the swim team is where you fit. Or, if you're not interested in physical activities, how about the math club or shop class? God has given you some super creative skills and natural talents. With your parents' permission, you'll want to try anything and everything until you find your special "thing."

> *Jesus grew in wisdom and stature, and in favor with God and men* (Luke 2:52). List the four areas of Jesus' development from a child to an adult. (And guess what? You need to grow in these same areas too!)

★ _____

★ _____

★ _____

★ _____

A Boy After God's Own Heart

Listen to your parents. By all means, listen to your parents! They know all about doing homework. They also know all about what it takes to be a student—the discipline, the effort, the hard work, the time, the faithfulness, and the commitment. So ask them what school was like for them. Ask them about their favorite subjects—and why. Ask them to tell you about their favorite teachers—and why. This will be one fun talk! You can even write down their answers right here.

My mom's/dad's favorite class in school, and why—

_____

_____

_____

My mom's/dad's favorite teacher in school, and why—

_____

_____

_____

I've said all through this book so far that you should do what your parents say. So, do your homework when they want you to do it. And be faithful to do it. Don't wait until they nag or threaten you. Do it without them asking. Taking care of your homework is one way to earn the privilege of being on a team or taking part in some after-school activities. And remember—sooner is better when it comes to getting your homework out of the way. As you read the verse below, think about how important learning and your daily schoolwork are.

Let the wise listen and add to their learning (Proverbs 1:5). What does the wise young man do?

_____

_____

_____

Straight Talk About Your Heart

Are you catching a glimpse of God's plan for you to learn and grow? Are you catching on that your schoolwork is an important part of your grand adventure through life? I hope you are.

But it's also important to realize that as a boy after God's own heart, your relationship with Jesus is the most important thing. It's a good thing to go to school, work hard, do your homework, and get good grades. Just be sure you are also taking care of your walk with Jesus. That's because "the Lord gives wisdom, and from his mouth comes knowledge and understanding" (Proverbs 2:6).

A Prayer to Pray

*Dear Jesus, I admit that I am not
too excited about school and schoolwork.
And I admit my attitude is pretty bad about
it most of the time.
But I get the big picture that
school is really important. I want
to grow in wisdom and knowledge
...like You did.
Amen.*

★ TRAVELING WITH JESUS ★

In this chapter we had some fun in God's Word learning about the importance of **S-C-H-O-O-L**. On this page, write out the point for each letter. (I'll get you started with "S.")

S—See school as a training ground for life

C_____

H_____

O_____

O_____

L_____

Now, write out one thing you liked, learned, or want to do about your time at school and doing your homework. Then enjoy the journey!

_____

_____

_____

_____

_____

A Boy After God's Own Heart

6

My Friends

Bart had been Dylan's best friend from the day Bart's family moved in next door. Both Bart and Dylan were five years old then. They started first grade together. They learned to read and write together. They had played games together. They were on the same little league teams each summer. They were inseparable buddies—until the day Jacob's family moved in down the street.

Dylan couldn't believe how many supercool video games and electronics Jacob had in his room. He was just one year older than Dylan and Bart, but he had every toy and game anyone could ever want! And Dylan couldn't believe that Jacob wanted to be *his* friend. Dylan had always considered himself a nobody. Jacob made him feel special, like a somebody.

But there were two problems with Dylan's friendship with the new kid down the block. First of all, Bart wasn't included, which meant Dylan had to make a choice between spending time with Bart or with Jacob.

The second problem was that Jacob had a mean streak. He treated Dylan okay, but the other kids in the neighborhood weren't so lucky, which included Bart. Jacob acted like he was way better than the other kids, maybe because he was a little older. But Dylan felt uncomfortable with Jacob's bad attitudes and actions. He was beginning to realize that if he didn't act like Jacob did, he would lose Jacob's friendship. Dylan was beginning to wonder if all of this was worth losing his good friend, Bart. He also didn't want to start becoming a neighborhood bully like Jacob.

Fun in God's Word!

Friends. Sometimes it seems like you can't live with them, and it sure seems like you can't live without them! They are definitely an important part of your life, aren't they? Friends make life more fun and interesting. They can help you grow in your communication skills as you talk and do stuff together. They can also help you develop many great character qualities. For example, with good friends, you learn the importance of telling the truth and not spreading rumors and gossip. And you also learn what it means to be loyal.

I'm sure you're seeing how important it is to be careful when and how you choose your friends. Your goal is to try to choose friends who help you to grow into a guy after God's own heart. And at the same time, you have to be a true and real friend to others.

Are you ready to work your magic with your pen as we see what God says about this important area of your life—F-R-I-E-N-D-S?

A Boy After God's Own Heart

Friends love at all times. Have you been in a situation like the one Dylan is in? Have you had to choose between a tried-and-true friend like Bart and a new friend? Maybe you and your longtime friend are now at different schools, and it's hard to stay close and connected.

When I was your age I had a best friend who lived just down the street from me. Like Dylan and Bart, we were best friends. We liked the same things, laughed at the same jokes, and shared the same love for sports—and for cheeseburgers and French fries! We were like twin brothers—always together. But then, when we went into middle school, we were no longer in the same classes. That meant we had to work hard to remain friends.

What did we do? We made sure to take the time to meet during the lunch break. And we made an effort to go to one or the other's house often. During the summer we made sure we signed up for the same baseball leagues. We tried hard to live out this verse from the Bible:

> *A friend loves at all times, and a brother [or sister] is born for adversity* (Proverbs 17:17). If your pen is handy, describe what a true friend does. When is a friend most needed?

_____

_____

_____

_____

Refuse to be a part of a clique. A clique is a group of people who spend all their time together and don't allow others to join them. At school or church, these are the boys or girls who sit together, walk together, talk to each other, and generally have nothing to do with anyone else. They may even dress alike in the same style of clothes.

Now, there's nothing wrong with having a group of friends that have some things in common. The problem comes when the group becomes mean and believes they are better than the outsiders.

Is this the kind of group you want to be a part of? I don't think so, even if (like Dylan) you consider yourself a nobody. Remember, you are a somebody to Jesus, even if you don't have any friends.

You can learn a lesson from Jesus. He was a friend to all, even "a friend of...sinners" (Luke 7:34). However, He was criticized because He ate and drank and talked with the "wrong" people—people who were rejected by others.

Like Jesus, you probably know how it feels to be avoided, ignored, excluded, and overlooked by others. So what can you do?

★ Grow in God, and you won't mind the cliques so much. Also, as you are growing in Christ, you will attract other friends who want to be more like Jesus.

★ Pray for God to bring a Christian friend into your life, and pray for the people in the mean group.

★ Be friendly to everyone, and be thankful for the friends you have. Also, be a true friend to your true friends!

Initiate friendships carefully. Choose your friends wisely. Why? Because you become what they are. That's why the Bible is very clear when it tells you what to look for in a friend—and also what to avoid at all costs. Your first goal is to seek out friends who are going in the right direction—toward Jesus. You should look for guys who will pull you along on your journey with Jesus. Where will you find friends like this? Usually you will find them at church or in Christian groups or activities.

> *He who walks with the wise grows wise, but a companion of fools suffers harm* (Proverbs 13:20). If your friends are wise, what happens to you? If your friends are fools, what happens to you?

_____

_____

_____

_____

Everyone deserves your friendliness. I hope you are getting God's message about how important it is to choose friends and friendships carefully. But don't forget you are to be friendly to all—like Jesus. What does it mean to be friendly? It's pretty easy. Just try living by the "Ten Commandments of Friendship."[1]

1. Speak to people—there is nothing as nice as a cheerful word of greeting.

2. Smile at people—it takes seventy-two muscles to frown and only fourteen to smile!

3. Call people by name—the sweetest music to anyone's ear is the sound of their own name.

4. Be friendly and helpful—if you would have friends, be friendly.

5. Be cordial—speak and act as if everything you do were a real pleasure.

6. Be genuinely interested in people—you can like *everyone* if you try.

7. Be generous with praise—cautious with criticism.

8. Be considerate of the feelings of others—it will be appreciated.

9. Be thoughtful of the opinions of others.

10. Be alert to give service—what counts most in life is what we do for others!

Nice is always in. So be nice. Have you ever heard of the Golden Rule? It says, "Do to others as you would have them do to you." Did you know that Jesus taught that?

(See Luke 6:31.) The Golden Rule is an important reason for being nice to others because we want them to be nice to us. But did you know that the Bible never tells us to just be nice? Here's what it says instead:

> *Be kind and compassionate to one another* (Ephesians 4:32). How are you to treat anybody and everybody?

_____

_____

_____

_____

Are you wondering, "So what's the difference between being nice, and being kind and compassionate?" Well, here it is. Being nice is just being polite. But being kind is being thoughtful and really caring about someone. As you probably know, you can "act" nice toward someone even when you really can't stand them. But being kind is a sincere action that comes from your heart. Here is another verse about being kind:

> *Love is patient, love is kind* (1 Corinthians 13:4). How do you show love to others?

_____

_____

_____

Don't gossip! Real friends don't tell secrets or spread rumors about their friends. A true friend is loyal and knows how to keep a secret. The Bible has a lot to say about gossip and how it harms friendships.

Whoever spreads slander is a fool (Proverbs 10:18). It's easy to get the meaning of this verse! Don't gossip and spread rumors about others. If you do, what does this verse say about you?

_____

_____

_____

A talebearer reveals secrets, but he who is of a faithful spirit conceals a matter (Proverbs 11:13 NKJV). What does a talebearer or a gossip do? What does a faithful friend do instead?

_____

_____

_____

If you've ever been hurt by gossip, you know the meaning of this proverb all too well. So don't gossip. You're supposed to be a *friend* to others, not someone who hurts others by sharing secrets or lies about them. To share a friend's secrets is to betray him. It will hurt your friendship. And guess what else? It will hurt you! Instead, you are to be loyal, trustworthy, and truehearted—a *real* friend.

Share Jesus with your friends. If you have a personal relationship with Jesus, then you have a friend in Jesus. He is the truest friend you could ever have and will ever have (John 15:15). Because Jesus is the best friend any guy could have, you want to tell others about Him, right? Briefly write out what Jesus means to you. Then pray for a chance to share with your friends what you have written.

_____

_____

_____

_____

_____

_____

_____

_____

_____

_____

Straight Talk About Your Heart

I hope you realize the importance of friends, and especially the right kind of friends. It's really important, because the right kind of friend will encourage you in the Lord. He will challenge you to grow spiritually and continue on your adventure with Jesus. In fact, he will be right there by your side enjoying the Jesus adventure together with you. And he will stay with you even during the tough times. So as you look for friends, start with prayer. Here's a prayer you can say. Or feel free to make up your own. Whatever you pray, say it from your heart.

A Prayer to Pray
Dear Jesus, please bring friends
into my life who will encourage me
and stand by me. Give me wisdom
and patience as I look for true friends.
Amen.

★ TRAVELING WITH JESUS ★

In this chapter we had some fun in God's Word learning about the importance of **F-R-I-E-N-D-S**. On this page, write out the point for each letter. (I'll get you started with "F.")

F—Friends love at all times

R_____

I_____

E_____

N_____

D_____

S_____

Now, write out one thing you liked, learned, or want to do about your friendships and being a better friend. Then enjoy the journey!

_____

_____

_____

_____

7

My Church

Wouldn't it be nice to sleep in just *one* day of the week?" Dylan said to himself as he turned over in bed to catch another snooze. But Dylan's mom was on the move! Sunday around his house was never going to be a sleep-in day. She was making the rounds, waking up Dylan and his brother and sister. Dylan groaned as he heard his mom's voice again: "Dylan? Dylan James! Get up N-O-W!"

He didn't want to, but Dylan rolled out of bed and staggered to the window. All was quiet in the neighborhood—at least, everywhere except at his house. Once the ordeal of getting up was over, however, Dylan smiled. It finally hit him—it's Sunday, Sunday at last! He had done something new for the first time on Saturday night—he had packed his Bible and Sunday school lesson and put them on his nightstand. Plus, to the amazement of his mom and dad, he had prepared himself by setting out his church outfit and even finding matching socks for his shoes!

Yes, each minute Dylan was getting more and more excited about going to church. This hadn't always been true. As with school, Dylan had just gone through the motions when it came to church. But recently, Sundays had started to become the highlight of his week. That's because of Brad, his new Sunday school teacher. Brad was a student at the local college. And Brad loved Jesus and enjoyed teaching the Bible to fifth- and sixth-grade boys. Brad's heart for the Lord had lit a spiritual fire in Dylan's heart. "Thank You, Jesus, for Brad!" Dylan prayed as he ran down the stairs to breakfast. Sunday at last!

Fun in God's Word!

At church, you can have fun with your friends and the other kids in your Sunday school class. And if you have a teacher like Brad, you can learn a lot about Jesus and about being a guy after God's own heart. Also, church is where you and your family can worship God together. In many ways, church is a good place to be!

Maybe you've had times when, on Sunday morning, you just don't feel like rising up and getting dressed to go anywhere. Who doesn't like lounging around in their pajamas and eating pancakes? But going to church is something God wants you and me to do. It's a great place to hear His Word, to learn about Him, and to learn about how He wants you to live.

Now it's time again for some more fun in God's Word. And you know what to do, right? Grab your pen and let's see what God has to say about your involvement at C-H-U-R-C-H.

Church is God's plan. In the Old Testament, God asked His people to worship Him in a specific place like a tabernacle (a tent) or a temple. But in the New Testament, God built His church out of people. So the church is not about a building. It's about a group of people who believe in Jesus as their Lord.

> *Christ loved the church and gave himself up for her* (Ephesians 5:25). How important is the church to Jesus?

_____

_____

_____

Have a positive attitude. There are so many good reasons to go to church. So it helps to go with a positive attitude. How? First, pray that you will pay attention. Also, listen and try to get as much as you can from the lessons taught by your pastor and Sunday school teacher. If a lesson was assigned in advance, be sure to do it. Then determine to participate in the discussion, to speak up at least once. And go to be friendly and to make new friends. Like you have already read, church is just a good place to be!

> *Worship the LORD with gladness; come before him with joyful songs...Enter his gates with thanksgiving and his courts with praise; give thanks to him and praise his*

name (Psalm 100:2 and 4). In these verses, circle at least four attitudes for worshiping God.

When you arrive at church and your youth group with an eager and open heart, you grow...and you please God. That's awesome!

Understand the importance of youth activities. Church is not school, and it's not home. It's a special place provided by God for His people—those who love Him—to get together.

Most churches have Bible clubs where you can play games, memorize Scripture, talk about Jesus, and have fun with other kids your age. Your church might also offer special day camps or weekend camps where you can get away and be with other kids and leaders who love Jesus. My personal favorite was our church's annual summer camp. I couldn't wait to go—the camp was next to a big lake, and had a gigantic swimming pool that was so much fun on those hot summer afternoons. And I really liked gathering together with the youth leader and the other kids to talk about the most important person in the world—Jesus! And how about winter camp? You get to stay in a cabin, roll around in the snow, build snowmen, go on nature hikes, and again, learn more about what it means to be a Christian.

So, if it is at all possible, don't miss out on these church activities. The things you do and learn, and the commitments you make during these times, can be some of the most important and memorable ones in your entire life.

Plus, you can begin some great, for-real friendships with other boys who follow Jesus too.

There's a story in the Bible that tells about a special time Jesus spent with His disciples. He told them:

> *Come with me by yourselves to a quiet place* (Mark 6:31). How does that verse encourage you to attend the next church youth activity (with your parents' approval, of course)?

_____

_____

_____

Reach out to other guys. Church is full of kids who love Jesus and want to know more about Him and the Bible. As the saying goes, "The ground is level at the foot of the cross." This means we are all the same when it comes to having a relationship with Jesus. In Christ, we are all one. Underline what the following verse says about how Christ makes us equal.

> *There is neither Jew nor Greek, slave nor free, male nor female, for you are all one in Christ Jesus* (Galatians 3:28).

Here are some things you can do to reach out to others in your group at church. Don't worry—these acts of friendliness are easy to do. All it takes to make them happen is your decision to do them!

★ Say hi to everyone—and smile.

★ Sit by any boy who is alone. And if you are with a friend, you can both go sit with him.

★ If someone is new or a visitor, be sure to say hello. Ask him where he lives and goes to school, or who he's visiting and how long he'll be there. Be friendly!

Christ is what church is all about. The focus on Jesus is what makes going to church different from going to school. It is His church. And you go there to learn about Him.

Your parents may talk about Jesus at home and have devotions together as a family. But church is another place where you can learn more about Jesus and His amazing life and miracles. You'll hear about His love and character qualities. You'll find out how He expects you to act and behave. You'll be blown away as you learn about what Jesus has done for you—that He died for you and your sin. And you'll hear about what it means to be a boy after God's own heart and enjoy eternal life in heaven forever.

Many Christians I know gave their heart and life to Jesus at church, where they discovered more about the Lord. The most important decision you will ever make is whether you will follow Jesus and give Him your heart and life. I'm praying that God will use His Word to open your heart to the truth of His love for you, and that you will respond to His invitation to "come to Me" (Matthew 11:28).

A Boy After God's Own Heart

In chapter 10, you will read more about becoming a Christian and what is at the heart of an adventure with Jesus. But for now, look at the verse below. What does it tell you about Jesus?

> *Jesus answered, "I am the way and the truth and the life. No one comes to the Father except through me"* (John 14:6).

_____

_____

_____

Help in any and every way. The church is sometimes called "the body of Christ." People in the body of Christ help each other—and you can help others too! If cupcakes are needed for your class at church or to raise money for kids to go to camp, ask mom if she can help you bake some. If help is needed to set up a classroom—or the nursery, or the sanctuary or auditorium—or to clean up afterward, ask mom and dad if it's okay to go a little early or stay a few minutes late so you can help out.

You can also help your parents with their ministries. I know a mom and dad who volunteer to take care of the babies in the church nursery—and their kids gladly help them after church is over. Their Jacob (age ten) helps by putting away the toys and equipment, rolling up rugs, and vacuuming the floor.

Or here's another way you can help. When there is a

church workday, ask your dad if you can go along with him. It's fun to plant and water flowers, sweep up leaves, and help make your church look nice.

Here's the goal: What you want is to develop a heart that serves. That is one way you can be more like Jesus. Read it for yourself:

Even the Son of Man did not come to be served, but to serve and to give his life as a ransom for many (Mark 10:45). What does this verse tell you about Jesus?

_____

_____

_____

Straight Talk About Your Heart

Dylan was glad and excited all week long as he waited for Sunday to come. He had Brad as a teacher—and he made being at church fun and exciting. But maybe you don't have a Brad. Remember that you are going to church to learn about Jesus. And when you do that, you will make Jesus happy.

Also, think of the neat things that happen to you while you're at church. For one, you are away from the world and its negative influences for a few hours. And you get to be in a place where the kids are thinking and talking about Jesus. Plus you can build friendships with other boys who have the same goals you have about growing as a Christian.

I hope and pray you love going to church. And if you're not very excited about the idea of going to church, I hope and pray you'll have a change of heart. Ask God to help you understand how important it is to meet with other Christians and grow in the Lord. And you can always pray to meet a new friend there, too—a brother in Christ, a friend and a boy after God's own heart you can look forward to seeing each week.

To sum things up, here are four good reasons to enjoy and appreciate your time at church. Each one is important, and each one is a great reason to want to attend church. You go to church…

—to worship Jesus.
—to be taught more about Jesus.
—to bring kids who need to know Jesus.
—to serve others like Jesus did.

A Prayer to Pray

Dear Jesus, it is time for me
to tell You how much I want
to know more about You.
And I want to know You as my Savior.
Help me to understand what
I am learning about You at church.
Amen.

★ TRAVELING WITH JESUS ★

In this chapter we had some fun in God's Word learning about the importance of **C-H-U-R-C-H.** On this page, write out the point for each letter. (I'll get you started with "C.")

C—Church is God's plan

H _____

U _____

R _____

C _____

H _____

Now, write out one thing you liked, learned, or want to do about your involvement at your church. Then enjoy the journey!

_____

_____

_____

_____

_____

A Boy After God's Own Heart

8

My Self

Wow! Oh, wow!" That was all Dylan could say. He was absolutely overwhelmed! He and his dad had just entered the civic auditorium, where the annual Backpacking Fair was being held. This was the first time Dylan's dad had invited him to the fair. (Well, his dad had invited him last year, but at the time he was more interested in goofing off with Bart and the neighborhood boys.)

But this year was different. Over the years, Dylan had watched his dad pack up his gear and drive off with some of his guy friends for a backpacking trip in the nearby state park. Up till now, Dylan had been too young to join his dad. Besides, it sounded like a lot of work to do all that hiking, so Dylan hadn't been all that interested. But now he was excited about learning how to go hiking like his dad. And he was especially glad to spend this special time together with his dad!

As Dylan stood inside the auditorium, he couldn't help but think about how things were changing in his life, his interests, his body, and his dreams. With each passing year, his schoolwork was getting more demanding. As his friends grew older and their lives changed too, it was becoming more difficult to have real friendships.

As for his body, it seemed like he was in a continuous growth spurt! His mom had trouble keeping him in clothes that fit. And his feet were getting so big! And strangely enough, as he grew older, things that used to be fun weren't quite so cool anymore. It seemed like life was getting more and more complicated.

Fun in God's Word!

Some parts of growing up are tons of fun. To begin with, there are lots of great new things to do almost every day. And as you grow physically, guess what? You get tall enough to go on more rides at the amusement park. You get better at sports, or whatever activities it is that you enjoy. And maybe you even need braces—which means you can choose some wacky color combinations for your bands every time you go to the orthodontist.

Yes, there are so many new things that can fill your days with adventure! And some of your new growth can be puzzling and even scary as your body changes and your responsibilities increase—like having more chores around the house. Or being asked to help watch your little brother or sister. Or staying at home alone until your parents return from work.

Well, good news! No matter what is happening now, God's Word has help, answers, and great encouragement for you as you continue your journey through life with Jesus. So prepare to discover some radical truths about your S-E-L-F. Here we go!

A Boy After God's Own Heart

Start each day with thanksgiving. It is a good thing to get into the habit of thanking God each new morning for His love for you. Do you realize there is never a minute in your life when you are not special to God and loved by Him? He made you. He knows everything about you. And He loves you—no matter what.

How does this help a boy who's busy growing up, a guy who is in the process of becoming a boy after God's own heart? Well, it helps to realize that, no matter what's going on at home with your parents and brothers and sisters, or at school, God loves you. Or when you feel like you're not very special—to yourself or to anyone else—you can know that you are a treasure to God and greatly loved by Him. Or when the kids at school aren't very friendly or nice, when it gets pretty lonely, you can always count on God's love for you. As you look at the following verses, let the fact that God loves you soak into your heart.

God so loved the world that he gave his one and only Son...(John 3:16). How great is God's love for His world and for you?

_____

_____

_____

_____

_____

God has said, "Never will I leave you; never will I for-sake you" (Hebrews 13:5). How strong and how long is God's love?

_____

_____

_____

Enjoy your life, yourself, and your days. One time while I was reading through my Bible, Psalm 118:24 really stood out to me. As I read it over and over and thought about the words, I made a decision. I decided that, before I even got out of bed each morning, I would begin each day with these words from Psalm 118:24 (NASB):

> *This is the day which the LORD has made;*
> *let us rejoice and be glad in it.*

You see, I had a bad habit. As soon as my alarm went off, I would start moaning and groaning and thinking, *Oh, no! Tell me it's not time to get up! Again? I'm so tired. Someone give me a break!*

But then I started acting on my decision to greet each new day with joy. So I would say these words in my heart or right out loud, no matter what was going on, no matter what I had to do that day:

> *This is the day which the LORD has made;*
> *let us rejoice and be glad in it.*

I chose to start each day by remembering God and being glad. Even if I had a big test to take, I made God my first thought. Even if I was sick, rejoicing in the Lord gave me a more joyful attitude. Even if I was going to the dentist (ugh!), I reminded myself that because God was in charge of my day, I could be happy.

Don't get me wrong. I really liked going to school. That's where my friends were. That's where my cool teachers were. That's where the action was. But there were always challenges. Like knowing my clothes weren't as fashionable as what the other guys were wearing, or I wasn't as clever as some of the other boys, or I wasn't as good at sports. Sometimes I wondered if anyone would play with me or hang out with me during lunch and recess. And there were times when I believed I was dumb when it came to math. (And never mind that I sometimes struggled to write a full sentence that was correct!)

Oh, there were lots of things I dreaded. Like being afraid I would give a wrong answer when the teacher called on me. Like taking the Friday spelling test. And there was stuff outside of school that I super dreaded—like my keyboard recitals. I loved music, and I even liked practicing and playing the keyboard. But the recitals were 100 percent pure dread.

Do you know what helped me through the hard things in my days? Psalm 118:24! No matter what was ahead in my day, remembering that "this is the day which the LORD has made" helped me to follow through on the rest of the verse: Therefore I will "rejoice and be glad in it." That's what helped to make a difference when things got tough.

The fruit of the Spirit is...joy (Galatians 5:22). What is a mark of a spirit-filled Christian who is walking by God's Spirit? Where does this quality come from?

_____

_____

_____

Look inside your heart, not at your outward appearance. I know that most guys would never admit that they might take an occasional peek at themselves in their mirror, right? Well, think about this: What if there were a secret timer hidden inside your mirror that recorded how much time you spend looking at yourself? What do you think the total number of minutes would come to each day?

And here's a more important question: What do you see when you look at yourself in a mirror? Most guys immediately see everything that's wrong with them—or what they *think* is wrong with them. They pass right by their good features and never even stop to notice! And instead, their eyes go straight to a nose they don't like, ears they think stick out, teeth they are sure will never straighten out. Their focus is on every blemish, every strand of hair that won't cooperate, or too many freckles.

Unfortunately, it is impossible to escape mirrors. But they do have a purpose: You can use them to make sure your appearance is neat, which sends the message that you are a boy after God's own heart—that you are neat, honest, reliable, innocent, and that you have a good attitude. But once you know you look okay, move on to real life. Thank God for what you are becoming—a growing guy who is more concerned about his heart and his character than his looks.

> *The LORD does not look at the things man looks at. Man looks at the outward appearance, but the LORD looks at the heart* (1 Samuel 16:7). How is the Lord different from people? Where do people tend to focus their attention? Where does God look instead?

_____

_____

_____

_____

Focus on what God says is good about you. In God and through Jesus, you are the object of His love. You are a trophy of His grace. If you have accepted Jesus as your Savior, then you are a member of the family of God. *This* is who you really are! No matter how you look or what abilities you have or don't have, you are priceless to Him. As you read the verse that follows, realize how God views you. And be sure to notice the attitude He wants you to have about who you are.

I praise you because I am fearfully and wonderfully made; your works are wonderful...(Psalm 139:14). God never makes a mistake. What do you learn here about yourself?

_____

_____

_____

Straight Talk About Your Heart

As I'm looking back over this chapter, my eyes are landing on words like *love, joy,* and *priceless.* These are words that speak of God's love for us. How great is that? Yet why is it that we think of ourselves so negatively when God is constantly telling us how priceless we are in His eyes? Why are we so hard on ourselves when God went to such great lengths—including the death of His Son Jesus on the cross—to shout out and show His love for us? Why do we put ourselves down when God is expressing how pleased He is with us?

Sure, sometimes we make mistakes. We mess up. We'll act unkind to someone, or we'll pay too much attention to what the "in guys" are wearing and want to dress like they do. And sometimes we get moody and pouty when things don't go our way.

But here's what's important to remember:

— Remember you are "fearfully and wonderfully made"—exactly the way you are. God Himself made you, and He never makes a mistake!

— Remember you can be joyful every second of every day—no matter what's happening to you—because God is with you.

— Remember you are in a constant state of change as you grow year by year. Some of these changes are new, so make sure you talk them over with your dad and mom.

— Remember you are as special as a one-of-a-kind snowflake, one of God's truly marvelous works!

Enjoy your journey with Jesus as you, like Him, grow "in wisdom and stature, and in favor with God and men" (Luke 2:52).

A Prayer to Pray
Dear Jesus, help me to remember
the great things I've learned about
Your love for me and the many ways
You are working in my life.
Life is always good...because of You.
Amen.

★ TRAVELING WITH JESUS ★

In this chapter we had some fun in God's Word learning about the importance of **S-E-L-F.** On this page, write out the point for each letter. (I'll get you started with "S.")

S—Start each day with thanksgiving

E_____

L_____

F_____

Now, write out one thing you liked, learned, or want to do about you and your self. Then enjoy the journey!

_____

_____

_____

_____

_____

_____

_____

A Boy After God's Own Heart

9

My Time

What a day!" Dylan muttered as he fell onto his bed. He usually hated to go to bed, but tonight he was feeling absolutely dog-tired. He could hardly wait to lie down, turn out his Darth Vader lamp, and finally get some sleep.

But just as Dylan was about ready to drift off to sleep, another thought jarred him—he hadn't spent time with Jesus today. His Sunday school teacher had challenged the boys in his class to take some minutes each day to read the Bible and pray.

"Oh, well," Dylan reasoned, "I just didn't have time today. And I'm too far gone now. I'll do it tomorrow. Well, at least I can say a quick prayer! It'll just have to do...'God, please bless me and my family...And, oh yes, God, bless my friend Bart too!'"

Yes, Dylan had done lots of activities earlier today. First there was school. Then after school there was a quickly organized ball game. Too bad Dylan's team was thoroughly trounced! Then there was a trip to the mall with his dad to pick up some supplies for their upcoming hiking trip. His day had been so packed that it seemed like he hadn't had any free time.

But as he thought about it, Dylan had to admit he had wasted some of his time. For starters, he had put off getting out of bed that morning. Which meant he had to rush out of the house to get to school on time. He had daydreamed his way through his study period at school. He had somehow managed to talk to all his friends throughout the day, and then poked his way through his homework in the evening, lingering by the TV each time he made a trip to the kitchen, and finishing his homework just in time to go to bed.

Even in what seemed like a hectic and busy day, Dylan could think of a lot of times when he could have taken a few minutes to do the most important thing in his day—spend some time with Jesus.

Fun in God's Word!

I think you and I can both identify with Dylan's tiredness. And we can also identify with his realization that life is very busy. There just doesn't seem to be enough T-I-M-E in a day to do everything we need to. So let's take a look at how we do spend our time, and how we can do better in this area of life.

Time is a treasure. You would never throw away treasures like money or gold or silver, would you? And, as a boy after God's own heart, you shouldn't throw away your days and minutes either. Why? Because they too are riches and treasures!

You may not think a lot about the value of your time and what you spend it on. But God says it is wise to realize how valuable time is. No one knows how long he or she will live, but we do know that we have today. And today is a treasure God has handed to you to spend and use wisely. How? Get your pen or pencil and see what God's Word says.

> *Teach us to number our days aright, that we may gain a heart of wisdom* (Psalm 90:12). What is the result when we value each day and pay attention to how we spend our time?

_____

_____

_____

It's important to "do it now." Do you have a bad habit of putting things off, especially if it's something you don't want to do? Your mom tells you to clean up your room, or do your homework. But you tell yourself, "I'll do it later." Or you have a test coming up at school. Your teacher has warned you in class every day for a week about this test. And still you haven't even started to study.

News flash! Guess what? Your messy room, your homework, and preparing for that test are not going to simply disappear into the misty realm of Neverland. Do you know what putting things off is called? *Procrastination*. That word means to delay doing something that needs to get done. We're procrastinating when we choose to put something off until later instead of doing it now. But God gives us a better way for getting things done. Read on!

I will hasten and not delay to obey your commands (Psalm 119:60). What words in this verse speak to the importance of doing things now?

_____

_____

_____

Make the most of your time. Dylan thought there weren't enough hours in the day to do all the things he had to do and wanted to do. What does God's Word say about this?

There is a time for everything, and a season for every activity (Ecclesiastes 3:1). This verse says there is a time for you to do all those things you want and need to do that are truly important.

Okay. Sometimes your days are jammed full of things you have to do. But here's another real-life scenario: You're at home...and it seems like there is absolutely nothing to do! No one's around to play with. You've completed your school-work on time (a miracle!) and all your chores are done (another miracle!). In fact, you've done about everything you can think of doing. So out of your mouth comes a big sigh and those dreadful words—"I'm bored."

Oh boy! Do you want to know the secret to never being bored again? Here it is: Make a list of "5 Things I Want to Do." The things you put on this list can include goals or dreams, hobbies, a series of books you'd like to read, or a new game or activity you want to learn.

Do you realize how truly exciting some free time could be? It gives you the opportunity to work on mastering a new skill or hobby. You can also write to a missionary or a pen pal or a friend who moved away. You can work on that model plane kit you received on your birthday. You can write and draw your very own comic book story. You can start on an adventure and begin reading great classic books like *The Swiss Family Robinson* or *Two Years Before the Mast.* You can even work on a personal Bible study that is just for you.

There are loads of things you can do and learn to do. You can get in some extra practice on your musical instrument. If you have a camera, you can spend this time taking pictures of your Lego creations, insects, and cool scenes. You can even read a library book on photography.

I know your parents determine how most of your time is spent. But you probably still have a lot of free time every day—time when you can choose what you do. It's easy to think about turning on the TV and vegging out (like Dylan did). And it is easy to fill your free time playing computer games you've played many times before. But once you make your "5 Things I Want to Do" list, you'll find there are some great new ways you can spend your time. You'll never again say, "I'm bored!"

As we've been learning, time is a treasure. And, like our verse said, we are to value each day and pay attention to how we spend our time. Use the five lines here to get yourself started on your list of...

Five Things I Want to Do

1._____

2._____

3._____

4._____

5._____

Evaluate your priorities. A priority is something that is more important than other things. There are many ways you can use your time. So, the question is, how can you begin to choose the *best* options over options that are not the best? How can you figure out what your priorities are?

Many of your activities—like school—have been decided for you by others. Other activities, like sports, music lessons, and going to church, have been established for you by your parents. Plus you have your chores at home. These priorities are set in stone. They are not going to budge or change. So how does God want you to approach these established priorities?

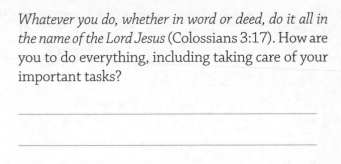

Whatever you do, whether in word or deed, do it all in the name of the Lord Jesus (Colossians 3:17). How are you to do everything, including taking care of your important tasks?

_____

_____

_____

If you don't do some planning (as Dylan discovered!), time with Jesus can easily get crowded out of your life. Now, Jesus does not want you to neglect school, family, or other important activities. But, just as you set aside time to go to school or practice a musical instrument, you need to set aside time to meet with God. After all, God is your Number One priority. That means you need to pick a time during the day when you will read His Word and pray. Spending time with the Lord is the most important priority you have every day. Look at these great verses and circle the word "seek" in each verse:

Seek first his kingdom and his righteousness (Matthew 6:33).

Blessed [happy] are they who keep his statutes and seek him with all their heart (Psalm 119:2).

I seek you with all my heart (Psalm 119:10).

O God, you are my God, earnestly I seek you (Psalm 63:1).

Straight Talk About Your Heart

I hope you are beginning to realize how important your time is, especially when it comes to time with Jesus. You make Jesus a priority when you make a commitment to spend time with Him... and follow through. Would you fail to show up for an appointment with a teacher? Would you skip a friend's birthday party? I don't think so! So why would you not make time for Jesus, the most important person in the world and in your life?

When you spend time with Jesus, great things happen. He makes your days more exciting. He gives you a happy heart. He helps you do your best and do it in a way that honors Him. He shows you how to be more kind and helpful to others. And He does His amazing work of transforming you into what you really want to be—a boy after His own heart. Then, when you put your head on your pillow at night, instead of feeling bad (like Dylan did), you can thank Jesus for a wonderful day!

A Prayer to Pray
Dear Jesus, I want to pay attention
to how I spend my time.
And most of all, I want to make sure
I spend time with You each day.
Amen.

★ TRAVELING WITH JESUS ★

In this chapter we had some fun in God's Word learning about the importance of **T-I-M-E.** On this page, write out the point for each letter. (I'll get you started with "T".)

T—Time is a treasure

I _____

M_____

E _____

Now, write out one thing you liked, learned, or want to do about how you spend your time. Then enjoy the journey!

_____

_____

_____

_____

_____

_____

10

My Journey with Jesus

What a trip! I can't believe all the important things we've talked about on our journey together with Jesus. I truly hope you've enjoyed our adventure. I know I have!

As we've traveled along, we have seen Dylan struggle with daily life at home, school, church, and with friends. (Could you relate?) We have looked at some of the key areas of a tween boy's life. We've also discussed what it means to be a boy after God's own heart—a boy who wants to know God and do His will.

Before we go our separate ways, here are a few key things to remember about Jesus and your heart and life. I'm sure you're not surprised that brings up another acrostic. Actually, it is a sentence. (And, of course, it spells J-E-S-U-S.)

Jesus, the Son of God,

Entered this world as a baby, and

Sacrificed Himself for sinners to

Unite them with the Father by

Securing eternal life for all who believe in Him.

Did you notice that throughout this book we have talked about Jesus and about being a Christian? Maybe you have been wondering, "What does it mean to be a Christian? Am I a Christian? How can I become a Christian?"

By now you are probably not surprised to know that the Bible tells us how to have a personal relationship with Jesus. Here are a few verses, often called "The Romans Road." That's because every verse on this "road" is from the book of Romans in the New Testament of the Bible.

The Romans Road

Romans 3:23 tells you about your sinful condition—*All have sinned and fall short of the glory of God.*

Romans 6:23 shows you the result of your sinful condition and reveals the gift God offers to you instead—*The wages of sin is death, but the gift of God is eternal life in Christ Jesus our Lord.*

Romans 5:8 points out God's grace and love for you and Christ's solution to your sinful condition—*God demonstrates his own love for us in this: While we were still sinners, Christ died for us.*

Romans 10:9-10 reveals some steps to take to become a Christian—*If you confess with your mouth, "Jesus is Lord," and believe in your heart that God raised him from the dead, you will be saved.*

I meet boys—and men—all the time who are not sure if they are a Christian or not. They want to be a Christian, but don't know how to become one. The way to make that happen is to receive Jesus Christ as your personal Savior. If being a Christian and becoming a child of God is the desire of your heart, you can pray a sincere prayer from your heart like this one:

A Prayer to Pray

God, I want to be Your child, a true boy after Your heart—a boy who lives his life for You, and not for himself. I admit that I am a sinner and often fail to do what You say is right. I receive Your Son, Jesus Christ, into my heart. I thank You that He died on the cross for my sins. Thank You for giving me Your grace and Your strength so that I can follow You with all my heart. Amen.

Straight Talk About Your Heart

As you finish this book and come to the end of this journey, guess what? It is not the end! That is because you will continue to walk with Jesus all through the rest of your life. You'll continue your journey with Him and grow more and more as the years pass by. For instance:

— You are going to grow in love—love for Jesus, love for your family, and love for others.

— You are going to grow in your knowledge of God's Word as you read your Bible, go to church, and surround yourself with friends who also love Jesus.

— You are going to grow in wisdom so you make fewer mistakes. You will learn what is right and what is wrong. And you will learn to make wise choices as you look in your Bible, pray, and talk with your parents and other Christians.

— You will grow in God's grace as you hit roadblocks or speed bumps on your journey and experience trials. But praise God, His grace is sufficient to see you through every problem and teach you how to handle them.

— You will grow in joy as you learn to love Jesus more and to walk closely with Him. He will strengthen you for every challenge. And you will know real joy as God blesses you for every victory, accomplishment, and achievement you experience by His grace.

God has great plans for you, my friend. Finishing this book is just one step toward knowing more about His plan. So congratulations on traveling to the end of this part of the journey to becoming a boy after God's own heart! Keep on keeping on. The adventures you will experience with Jesus have only just begun!

Note

1. Roy B. Zuck, *The Speaker's Quote Book* (Grand Rapids, MI: Kregel, 1997), p. 159.

Books by Jim George for Teen Boys

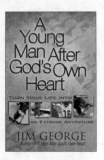

A Young Man After God's Own Heart

Pursuing God really is an adventure—a lot like climbing a mountain. There are all kinds of challenges on the way up, but the awesome view at the top is well worth the trip. This book helps teen guys to experience the thrill of knowing real success in life—the kind that counts with God. (This book was a 2006 Gold Medallion Award Finalist.)

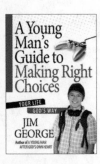

A Young Man's Guide to Making Right Choices

This book will help teen guys to think carefully about their decisions, assuring a more fulfilling and successful life. A great resource for gaining the skills needed to face life's challenges.

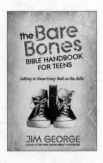

The Bare Bones Bible® Handbook for Teens

Based on the bestselling Bare Bones Bible® Handbook, this edition includes content and life applications specially written with teens in mind! They will be amazed at how much the Bible has to say about the things that matter most to them—their happiness, friends and family, home and school, and goals for the future. Great for youth group studies!